Beer, Hope a

Hewitt's Grimsby Br(

To Stephen
Best wishes
Graham Larn
(2009)

Graham Larn
foreword by Peter Chapman

Century Zero Four

2

Published by Century Zero Four Publications
185 Rutland Street
Grimsby
North East Lincolnshire DN32 7ND
email: hewittsbook@lycos.co.uk

ISBN 978-0-9560914-0-6

British Library Cataloguing in Publication Data. A catalogue record for this book is available from the British Library.

Printed and bound in Great Britain by Spectrum Print, Cleethorpes

Editors: Dennis Lister and Martin Clausen
Cover design and layout: Martin Clausen
Illustrations: Bill Tidy and Abigail Zambon
Title page illustration: Hewitt's Brewery gates, p. 4: William Hewitt (Abigail Zambon)

Contents

Dedicated to the people who worked for Hewitt's

Foreword

A day or two before joining the army 52 years ago my abstinent grandfather made me promise him that if I was ever to have an alcoholic drink it would be beer ... and nothing else.

He knew that his lifelong teetotalism was not the way for my generation. And so he made me promise. And I did. I am still keeping the promise.

I feel quite sure the beer he had in mind was Hewitt's. For although he had no experience of it, it had a reputation for being weak - a boy's beer, the sort of beer one could have more than one pint of without dire results.

And he was right. And at least three generations of Grimsby and Cleethorpes (and beyond) people probably had their first pint in one of Hewitts' innumerable houses. And they were not the worse for it. And it made a very good ginger beer shandy too.

I am flattered to be asked to write the foreword for this welcome and worthwhile history of Grimsby's own brewery.

For its houses were hospitable places and the family which owned them generous to the town which had made them a fortune.

It is not true that Grimsby's businessmen of yore were selfish.

But however permanent they must have appeared the houses have passed and Hewitts is no more.

But for those of us who recall the old days we do so with the happiest of memories.

And I remain grateful for wise advice ... and the making - and keeping - of promises.

Peter Chapman, summer 2008

Introduction

Mention Grimsby to anyone from outside the town and people will immediately reply "Fish!" It is still the centre of the fish processing industry, although for reasons not of its making, the trawler fleet has been decimated and the fish imported. Of course, one couldn't deny that when the wind was in the right (or should that be wrong?) direction there was a certain odour in the air. From another quarter there was the smell from the cow hide works but pervading the town centre there were two very pleasant odours indeed. Firstly, the bitter sweet smell of marmalade production from Tickler's jam factory and just a little way down the same street, the fabulous scent of malt and hops from Hewitt's brewery.

Unfortunately, both these firms have long departed and the town is the poorer for that in more ways than one.

My daily bike ride home from school would at one time take me past the brewery. It was always wreathed in steam and many are the times that I had had to wait whilst barrels were rolled across the street from the cooperage for filling. The drays were a familiar sight and it seemed that every pub had the brewery's sign, since it had a virtual monopoly. If you didn't like their beer, you had to go out of your way to find an alternative.

Like most Victorian buildings, the premises had some character, unlike the law courts which have taken over the site but for the present, a small part remains. That cooperage is still there, although in a state of dereliction and desperately seeking alternative use.

A remarkable survivor; so enjoy its presence whilst you can, as I indeed hope that you will enjoy the following pages outlining the story behind one of Grimsby's erstwhile premier brewers.

Dennis Lister, secretary
Campaign for Real Ale, Grimsby branch, spring 2008

Part 1 - Hewitt's story

Remember the days when there were lots of "local firms for local people"? Names like Tickler's Jam, Granville Tours, Eskimo Frozen Foods, Dixon's Paper Mill, Lawson and Stockdale, Partington's Yeast Merchants and of course Hewitt's Brewery were on everybody's lips. Now, sadly they are all gone.

I am often asked "What was Hewitt's beer like?" Well, to use one of my late father's expressions, "I was but a surly teenaged schoolboy" when Hewitt's ceased brewing in 1968 and so never drank the original brew. However, I did try the recently recreated offering a time or two and I'm told by seasoned drinkers that it was possibly better than the Pasture Street version.

Early years (19th century until 1910)

It is not common knowledge but Hewitt's did not originally brew on Grimsby's Pasture Street. This latter site was founded by J Garniss, who built the small brewhouse in September 1806. In March 1807, the first barrel of beer was rolled out but by 1810, Garniss had sold the business to John Hobson. From here, things become a little unclear. It is suggested by some sources that Hobson went on a spending spree, buying every pub in Grimsby; thus giving the town's drinkers "Hobson's

Choice" in their choice of beer. However, others suggest that it was the Hewitt brothers who in later years embarked upon a buying rampage.

Unlike today's world where everything has to be accounted for, 200 years ago things were less so and consequently information which would be of interest to us today was not recorded - it would have been deemed unnecessary to do so. Unfortunately, it does leave some black holes in our story.

John Hobson ran the brewing operation in Pasture Street, seemingly as the sole owner until his death on 5th January 1871. However there appears to be some speculation that Hobson actually sold it pre-1871 to E Smith & Co., who were subsequently taken over by Tower Brewery Co. of Tadcaster, Yorkshire and perhaps he retained some sort of ownership of the site itself. Therefore it could be explained how Hobson's interests in the brewery were held by trustees William Dann and John Herringshaw upon his death.

The business was then acquired by William Taylor Hewitt and Thomas Hewitt, trading as "Hewitt Brothers". Officially purchasing the brewery in 1874, there is a suggestion that they had started operating a year or two earlier, for in 1871, William was recorded as residing at 6 Pasture Street, Grimsby with his wife and three children, governess Elizabeth Darling and a general servant, a Miss Barratt. His occupation was described as "Brewer".

William Taylor Hewitt (artistic impression by Abigail Zambon)

William Taylor Hewitt was born in Tuxford, Nottinghamshire in 1832 and not in Bawtry, Yorkshire as some publications suggest. He did however reside in Bawtry, where he ran a wines and spirits business. In 1864, the year that his youngest child, Titus was born, he moved to Grimsby to operate a grocery shop in the Old Market Place (now Chambers Bar). Disillusioned by being a mere shopkeeper, he decided that his future was in brewing. Since most of his family were in that business, then so should he be.

As already mentioned, in 1874 William formed a partnership with his brother Thomas, in order to purchase the Tower Brewery. A further brother, Edwin took over the Exchange Brewery in Doncaster and ran it from 1878 until 1880, when he moved to the Springfield Brewery in Yeadon near Leeds, although there is evidence of an Edwin Hewitt (thought to be his son) running a brewery in Hull.

Another brother, John Henry Hewitt owned the Ordsall Brewery in Retford and Trent Brewery in Gainsborough. All of these companies were eventually acquired by the Grimsby operation.

William's wife, Elizabeth died on 9th August 1884, aged 53. Despite this major upset in his life, he carried on with his business interests and in 1888, a private limited company was formed in the style of "Hewitt Brothers Limited", with an original share capital of approximately £200,000. In Victorian times, this was of course a huge amount of money, with most of the shares being held by the Hewitt family. Sadly, William's brother Thomas died shortly after the company was formed, leaving William to go it alone.

WT Hewitt was a very shrewd businessman and had the brewery built on a grander scale. It was said at one time to be the tallest building in Grimsby; second only to the Dock Tower and the boardroom and offices were reputed to be amongst the most luxurious in the country. Under his guidance, the firm grew and grew – taking over in 1891 the brewing interests of Gale's Humber Brewery, which stood near to the Bull Ring in the town centre and purchasing any pub going. Much of his success was due to his down-to-earth approach to the business. These days it would be called "hands on" – something sadly lacking in today's workplace.

The Pasture Street Brewery – original premises marked with box

It is reputed that William drove around the local area in a horse and cart, persuading publicans to buy his beer, rather than to go to the trouble of brewing it themselves, as in those days, many pubs brewed on the premises, usually in a backroom or an outhouse. His hard work paid off and Hewitt's soon had a fleet of horse drawn drays (carts), delivering over a wide area.

After residing for a short period in the original brewery house facing onto Pasture Street he bought Weelsby Old

Hall. The Old Hall was virtually in the country at that time but was closer to the centre of Grimsby when destroyed during World War II.

Early 20th century photo of The Globe (possibly Nelson Street, Grimsby)

William lived a modest lifestyle there with his family until his death on 8th April 1902, aged 70. His business empire and vast fortune was inherited by his one

Page sponsored by Wollaston Road Stores, Cleethorpes

daughter, Mary Elizabeth and two sons, Henry Titus and Thomas William Good Hewitt.

AN OBITUARY
From the Grimsby Observer 10th April 1902
DEATH OF MR. W.T.HEWITT, J.P.

The death took place on Tuesday, of Mr. William Taylor Hewitt, J.P., at his residence, Weelsby Old Hall, near Grimsby. Deceased, who was about 70 years of age, was the principal in the large brewery firm of Hewitt Bros., Ltd., Tower Brewery, Grimsby. For the past two or three months, Mr. Hewitt had been very ill and of late in a very critical condition. He took no active or prominent part in public life, doubtless due to the extensive expansion of the business of the firm of late years. In 1877, Mr. Hewitt entered the Council and retained the seat until November 1885, when he retired. From that year he did not again seek municipal honours. Deceased was a justice of the peace for the Bradley-Haverstow Division of Lincolnshire and for some years a Guardian of the Poor. Though Grimsby cannot claim deceased as a native, he had passed the greater part of his life in the town. Deceased took up his residence at Weelsby Old Hall about twelve years ago, previously the family seat of Mr. Thorold Grant-Thorold. Politically Mr. Hewitt was a Conservative. He leaves two sons and a daughter.

Titus, who was a lawyer, kept one eye on the firm's Doncaster area and was a rare visitor to Grimsby, preferring a country squire type of life, thanks to his father's diligence. He was also interested in flying long before it caught people's imagination and may have been because on 17th October 1898 Titus was involved in a railway accident. The Grimsby to Manchester passenger train in which he was travelling (first class of course!) was approaching Wrawby Junction, near Barnetby, Lincs, when some huge timbers on a badly loaded goods train from the opposite direction slipped and sliced through the roofs of his train's coaches. Titus had witnessed the whole catastrophe through his window. He was not injured and assisted rescuers with the injured and dying, an experience which he never forgot.

Interior of The Honest Lawyer; Betsy Bentinck, landlady on left (circa 1905)

He died in 1910 aged 46 years, leaving the whole of the Hewitt Bros. Empire to his brother Thomas William Good. Their sister Mary died aged 50 in October of the following year, having moved to and lived in Henley-on-Thames for many years.

The Thomas Hewitt era (1910 to 1930)

Thomas William Good Hewitt (TWG), son of William and not to be confused with Thomas, his uncle and co-founder of the brewing company, took the reins in 1910. His duty to the company is legendary, as is his devotion to his workforce and to the town that made his family's fortune. Said to be a stern but fair employer, he was to be found in his office virtually everyday. He made a point of making personal contact with all of his staff; always approachable and ready to help with any problems that they may have had. Many of his staff stayed for years, with some notching-up 50 years service. TWG, like his father was "hands-on" with all aspects of the business. He would sample and purchase the barley himself. Malt samples were taken to him each morning and various grades of beer were tasted by him every day. He had the reputation of being an excellent beer taster.

The 1926 "Great Strike" (also referred to as the General Strike) followed the sacking and "locking out" of miners. Thousands of British manual workers downed tools and refused to work, all Britons in employment were asked to support the miners by also going on strike. Hewitt's Brewery staff were preparing to follow the rest of the country in withdrawal of labour, when Thomas had a meeting with the leaders of the workforce. He quietly put one simple question to them, which gave them pause for thought. Within a short period of time, all of his employees had returned to their normal working duties. It has to be left to people's imagination what exactly was said.

Thomas William Good Hewitt, courtesy Grimsby Telegraph

A great lover of horses, he purchased them personally for the drays. No whips were allowed to be used and the horses had regular rest periods in the grounds of Mr Hewitt's home. Other interests were collecting fine art, growing prize-winning flowers and he was a keen book reader. He was rarely seen in public and was driven to work in an enclosed buggy but he did a lot for the townsfolk of Grimsby and Cleethorpes. Apart from being Chairman and Managing Director of Hewitt's, he was also Chairman of the board of the Palace Theatre; a member of Grimsby Rural District Council and a genuine supporter of local charities. Anybody with a just cause was usually listened to and supported by Thomas. A vast landowner both locally and in Buckinghamshire, he donated large tracts of land to the local authorities in the interests of road safety; Hewitt's Avenue, Hewitt's Circus and Hewitt's Manor being a case in point.

Thomas died on 9th May 1930. His funeral was akin to a royal occasion and the cortege was said to be a quarter-mile long. Old Clee Church was swamped with mourners; a similar scene being witnessed at Cleethorpes Cemetery, where hundreds came to give their respects. Many had lined the route on the way there. He was laid to rest in the same plot as his parents and the memorial can still be seen today, although in a bad state of repair, with the inscriptions barely readable – a sad end to a family who gave so much to the town. He left many gifts in his will to employees: £10,000 to a fund for 1914-18 war officers; £3,000 to Clee Grammar School for a scholarship fund and

£20,000 to Grimsby Hospital. The bulk of his fortune went to Vivian, son of Titus, as he had no children of his own to bequeath to. Be warned and make a will of your own.

The memorial of William, Elizabeth and Thomas WG Hewitt
on Cleethorpes Cemetery (photo by the author)

Page sponsored by The Mini Market, North Sea Lane, Humberston

The modest millionaire (1930 to 1934)

Vivian Vaughan Davies Hewitt inherited the bulk of his late uncle Tom's fortune in 1931. It included the brewery, the Palace Theatre, over 300 pubs, hotels, parts of Grimsby docks, areas of land, Weelsby Old Hall and a huge amount of money that made him a millionaire. Captain Vivian as he was to be known, was something of a rich playboy. Not in the style of the 1970's television characters Jason King, played by Peter Wyngard, or The Persuaders aka Roger Moore and Tony Curtis (younger readers ask your parents!) but as a racing car enthusiast and literally a high flyer, as he carried on his father Titus' interest in aviation.

Vivian's father moved his family to Wales in their younger days. It was his mother Julia's homeland and it was here that the Captain put down his roots; virtually turning his back on Grimsby.

Despite being part of a wealthy family, Titus had insisted that his son should be able to earn a living on his own. Vivian was sent off to Harrow – a high seat of education. Upon leaving there, he embarked on a world tour to further educate himself and later went to work in Portsmouth Dockyard. Moving on to Crewe in Cheshire in order to work as an apprentice in the railway works, he later went on to run his own engineering business, dealing with cars and aircraft at Brooklands. He already owned many racing cars and planes by this time.

Page sponsored by No 2 Pub (Under the clock), Cleethorpes Railway Station

Vivian Hewitt's flight to Dublin: before take-off in Holyhead, 1912
(from collection of Peter Chapman)

At the age of 24, the Captain was plunged into instant fame. In spring 1912 he became the first person to fly across the Irish Sea; leaving Holyhead in Wales and arriving in Dublin 75 minutes later. It was also the longest flight ever made over water up to that time. The Irish press went into raptures with one headline stating "Grimsby Gentleman's Nephew Aeroplanes Across Irish Sea" and a wonderful quote from a Dublin butcher who was one of the first to witness the historical event, who said "I though it was a huge bird that was paying Dublin a visitation but soon tumbled to the startling fact that it was a wonderful machine with a man in it." Vivian went on to explain to the crowd which had gathered in the city's Phoenix Park, how he had navigated the flight at a height of 300 feet in thick fog without a compass. "I find that they don't work at high altitudes" he said, continuing "My only nasty moment occurred above the

Page sponsored by www.fulstowbrewery.co.uk

Guinness Brewery when my speed was reduced to 20 mph and I thought my flight was going to end in the (River) Liffey".

Vivian Hewitt (1888 – 1965) in his early 30s (from collection of Peter Chapman)

Page sponsored by Shop! Brookenby Village, Lincolnshire

In the First World War Vivian served in an ambassador-like function for Great Britain in the USA, overseeing quality control of the manufacture of aircraft that were built for Britain. Eventually, a bad accident ended Vivian's flying days for good. Arriving back in Rhyl after World War I, he discovered new interests. He began collecting birds' eggs; gradually becoming a strong conservationist many years before it was a trendy thing to do. He purchased an isolated house plus a piece of coastline at Cemlyn in Anglesey and established a bird sanctuary there.

Like his father, he was not interested in the brewing business, so he immediately put his inheritance up for sale. By 1934, Hewitt's had been sold and formed into a public limited company – these days referred to as a plc, but more on that story later!

Although Vivian took most of Grimsby's beer money away with him, he did however pay £1400 for restoration of the chancel in Old Clee Church, which in 1935 was at the point of total collapse. Thus ended the Hewitt family's direct generosity to the local townsfolk.

As he grew older, Vivian became more and more reclusive, with only a handful of close friends that he would trust. He is alleged to have become very crotchety, eccentric and oddly behaved – spending thousands of pounds on rare birds, including two stuffed Great Auks. He eventually moved to the Bahamas, leaving behind the damp weather and high taxation but retaining the bird sanctuary. Continuing to collect almost anything – stamps, butterflies etc., his collections were much revered by experts. Vivian suffered from cancer and died during a visit to Cemlyn in 1965 at the age of 77. His ashes were scattered in the bird sanctuary which is still there to this day.

Expansion: Hewitt Bros. Ltd. (1934 to 1961)

1934 – the year that Hewitt's came into public ownership, with major financial institutions coming on board. A merchant bank as well as brewers Bass, Ratcliff & Gretton, Worthington & Co. and Whitbread & Co. all had substantial shareholdings in the Grimsby firm. However, there was a hint of scandal arising in June of that year, when it was alleged that some insider dealing, as it is referred to today, had taken place in the stock market. A charge was laid against an agent at London's Bow Street Magistrates Court, concerning the theft of an internal balance sheet analysis of the brewing company, showing a list of interested parties which he took from his employers to another agent, who then went on to make a huge profit. The flotation, of course went ahead. Sir James Calder was appointed to the board of directors as the new chairman. He came from a large Scottish brewing company and was highly respected throughout the brewing industry. Under his leadership, Hewitt's expanded greatly, thanks to the injection of public money - one of the advantages of being a plc.

There is of course a downside to going public, as we shall learn later on.

Sergeant's Brewery, Brigg, 1920's (courtesy Grimsby / NELC library)

Hewitt's had, in 1922, under the ownership of Thomas Hewitt, purchased the brewing business of Messrs Norton & Turton Ltd. of 5 Drury Lane, Lincoln and under the stewardship of Sir James Calder, they went on to acquire the much revered AM & E Sergeant's brewery of Brigg in Lincolnshire. It is unclear when this purchase actually occurred - there are conflicting reports stating that Sergeant's was taken over either in 1937, 1945 or 1954. Whichever date the occasion was, Hewitt's, in their wisdom kept the Brigg Riverside operation open; installing new plant and push-button control systems, since Sergeant's beers were considered "as nectar" by steelworkers in nearby Scunthorpe. The tiny Brigg brewery was closed circa 1964 and brewing of Dolphin Ales was transferred to Grimsby. From then on the Sergeant's brands quickly disappeared to be replaced by Hewitt's Grimsby Ales.

Hewitt's, now operating as a publicly owned company, went from strength to strength. They expanded rapidly by building their own maltings on Grimsby's Victoria Street (now modern shop units), enlarging the cooper's building and extending the bottling plant in Queen Street. Eventually Hewitt's took over the entire block of buildings, including a disused Methodist Chapel. They also bought up dozens of public houses, locally and regionally.

There were dark clouds on the horizon in the shape of World War II because during World War I, restrictions on beer production, pub opening hours and strength of beer were made very strict, as was taxation on ale, said to pay for the war effort. However, taxes were not reduced when the war ended.

When World War II broke out in 1939, restrictions were again brought in. Hewitt's like all breweries in Britain were affected. Beer strength was reduced, taxation increased and inferior ingredients were forced to be used. Flaked maize, flaked oats and in 1943 even flaked potato was used to replace malt and the hopping of ale was reduced by 20% on normal usage. The call to war meant that women were to be employed again in the brewing industry doing manual work and a fine job they did too, emptying hops into brewing vessels, shifting barrels and helping load the drays. Motor delivery lorries were commandeered by the British army. Beer glasses were in short supply with rumours of pubs dispensing ale into jam jars! Bottles of beer were sold without labels in order to conserve paper. With no rationing of beer, unlike with food, consumption actually went up and consequently, pubs were forced to close on one day per week in order to conserve supplies.

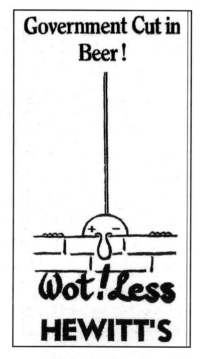
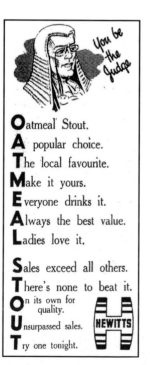

Different styles of Hewitt's advertisements (left: 1946, right: 1955)

At the end of the war and for a number of years to come, Hewitt's, like everyone, had restrictions placed upon them. Production had to be reduced and alcoholic strength lowered on all beers. With the country almost bankrupt and with food rationing still in force, signs were displayed outside pubs saying "SORRY NO BEER!" and brewers blamed "girls" for drinking beer instead of cocktails, causing a beer shortage. Amazingly, despite heavy bombing on the town, with its high tower and close proximity to the commercial and fish docks, the brewery buildings were largely untouched by enemy action, something that town planners in later years would put paid to. Things finally improved for people and the business in the 1950's, rationing eventually ceased in 1953, with sweets being the last commodity but things were to change in brewing and Hewitt's in particular.

Delivery of malt to the brewery, late 1940's

During the war years, draught beer had become rather unreliable in taste and quality. In this period, drinkers were ordering more bottled beers, because they were more consistent in quality and tasted indeed rather fresher. Beer in bottle was more expensive than that from the pump, so in order to save a shilling or two, customers would buy a half-pint of draught and a half-pint of bottled beer, thus creating the "pint of mixed", "brown and mild", "light and bitter" and other combinations of cask and bottled drinks. All helped to liven up beer that was stale and lifeless.

Racking Hewitt's XXXX Mild into barrels

The upsurge in packaged beer after the Second World War was phenomenal and consisted mainly of the bottled variety (there were not many canned beers around in those days) and this demand for bottled ales prompted Hewitt's to expand its bottling plant and variety of its packaged products. Nationwide, drinkers couldn't get enough of these take-home ales, resulting in Hewitt's commencing to bottle drinks on behalf of the big brewers, which included Bass & Co. and Arthur Guinness of Dublin.

After the war these bottle filling arrangements were something of a lifeline to regional brewers such as Hewitt's. Being a well-run business, the company went on to purchase public houses in Yorkshire, including one in the Tinsley district of Sheffield.

In 1956, Donald Burt, Hewitt's Managing Director, announced a "big deal", in which Hewitt Bros Ltd. had made an arrangement with EF Flower & Sons, brewers of Stratford-upon-Avon, Warwickshire, to purchase over 30 public houses in Louth, Alford, Horncastle and surrounding districts in mid-Lincolnshire. These were originally owned by Soulby Sons & Winch of Louth and Alford and acquired by Flowers in 1951, when the Stratford firm bought out the Lincolnshire brewers.

(Historical note: The brewery of EH Soulby & Sons of West Street, Alford was still standing in 2008, albeit in a derelict state, awaiting either restoration or demolition. It was built in the 1840's and is situated behind the White Horse pub, which was what is known as the "brewery tap").

Hewitt's purchase of the pubs for an undisclosed sum was claimed to be one of the biggest deals that the company had made. "We do not mind where we go but we will remain a local brewery" said Mr Burt and continued "Our business will not expand to the South of the country."

Page sponsored by High Spirits Shop & Off-License, Chelmsford Ave, Grimsby

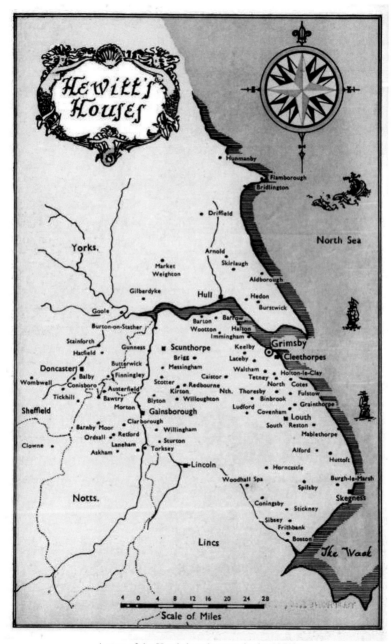

A map of the Hewitt's pub estate in the 1950's

Aerial view of Grimsby's St James Church and Bullring area circa 1960 - note Hewitt's building (former Gale's Humber Brewery) and Overbeck house (white front) top right corner, courtesy Grimsby Telegraph

The 1950's marked a period of prosperity for Hewitt's but as the decade was drawing to a close, a rather gloomy future was emerging for the brewery. In April 1959, Sir James Calder had tendered his resignation as Chairman and Director of the firm. He was 89 years old when he stepped down and had been in charge since 1934, when Hewitt's became a public company following the death of Thomas William Good Hewitt in 1930. In a letter to holders of ordinary shares, he stated that voting control had passed to a financial group which wanted to make changes to the board. Two other board members resigned at the same time as Sir James: Mr R.A.N. Shute and

Major J.D. Wigan did so for the good of the firm, allowing the money men a more coherent board of directors.

The new Chairman was Michael Richards, who was also chairman and director of merchant bankers Hart, Son & Co. He was, in addition made a director of Hewitt's. It was alleged that Hart, Son & Co. had built up a substantial holding in the brewery - £500,000 of ordinary stock, amounting to about 45% interest in the company.

A new decade ... and a bright new world was emerging. It was the start of the "swinging sixties". Conservative Prime Minister Harold McMillan had already told the country "You've never had it so good!" but things were not looking so good in the brewing industry. We were now entering what is considered "The Golden Age of British Television". Series like Sunday Night at the London Palladium, The Forsyte Saga, The Avengers, The Prisoner, Coronation Street and even Thunderbirds were luring people away from pubs and clubs. This problem coupled with the fact that a giant drinks industry predator was emerging from across the Atlantic Ocean (Canada to be precise) and was putting great fear into brewery owners.

Takeover – the years from 1961

Edward Plunket Taylor was an industrialist from Canada who had started a brewing empire in his homeland and in the USA. In 1930, ironically the year that Thomas Hewitt had died, one of Taylor's first purchases was that of Carling Breweries Ltd. of London, Ontario, which had been founded in 1843 by an expatriate Yorkshireman, Thomas Carling. The brewery had produced a beer called Black Label Rice Beer since the early 1920's, the name was shortened to Black Label in 1927. The Carling Brewery was closed in 1936 and brewing of Black Label was transferred to another of Taylor's operations. EP Taylor formed Canadian Breweries Ltd. and went on to take a dominant role in the Canadian and American brewing industry. His ambition was to do the same in the UK.

In October 1959, Taylor established a company called Northern Breweries Ltd., in which he could fulfil his dream of conquering British brewing and pushing Carling beer on the UK market. He purchased John Jeffrey & Co. of Edinburgh, followed by Hammond's of Bradford and Sheffield's Hope & Anchor. By the close of 1960, Northern had snapped up six English and five Scottish breweries, one in Wales and one in Belfast. By now he had changed the name to Northern United Breweries and at the same time, Carling Black Label had started to appear in pubs of the UK.

Page sponsored by Smugglers Pub, High Cliff, Cleethorpes

Moors & Robson building, Hull in 1984, note Bass triangle (picture: Pete Milsom)

During 1960, word in the trade about the Canadian brewer's planned dominance spread like wildfire. In April of that year, Hewitt's, together with Moors & Robson of Hull announced that they were to merge. It was a mutual attempt to avoid being taken over by Taylor's group. Since the Grimsby firm was the larger of the two and had a bigger shareholding in the merged group it was in effect an acquisition of Moors & Robson by Hewitt's. Both firms retained their own identity and their own breweries. However it was something of a stay of execution, because in December 1961, Hewitt's and its subsidiaries fell to Northern United Breweries for the sum of £7.5 million. *(Historical note: a similar takeover of the family-owned Hardys & Hansons Kimberley Brewery near Nottingham in 2006 by brewers Greene King of Bury St. Edmunds was priced at around £231 million. Kimberley was a similar sized company to Hewitt's).*

Northern United Breweries merged with Charrington's in 1962 and in 1967, 'Charrington United' had merged with Bass to form Bass-Charrington and took lots of local and regional breweries, including Hewitt's into its ownership.

Blundell Park, Grimsby Town FC football ground in Cleethorpes, 1960 (courtesy Grimsby Telegraph)

Moors & Robson (M&R) had ceased brewing, closed in 1964 and the brewery was demolished later that year. Their beers were recreated at Hewitt's for the Hull region and M&R's pubs, as with Sergeant's of Brigg which were rebadged into Hewitt's outlets. Gordon Robson, great-grandson of Edward Robson, one of M&R's founders, became MD of Hewitt's in 1977, succeeding

Peter Hewitt, a descendant of the Hewitt family. Mr Hewitt became Chairman of Canada Dry drinks division and Mr Robson went on to be Sales Director Licensed Houses, Hewitt Bros. Ltd., based in Hull and later became MD of William Stones Ltd. of Sheffield. He retired in 1989 aged 54.

During the early to mid-1960's, to business outsiders things seemingly carried on as normal, with Hewitt's continuing to support local charities and causes, which included sponsoring the "Mariners" (Grimsby Town Football Club), in the true spirit of the brewery's founders, William and Thomas. However as the so-called "Summer of Love" (1967) progressed, rumours were again flying around the industry of consolidation within the brewing companies. Bass, who now of course owned Hewitt's, had too many members in its family, so some would have to leave the nest. With the upsurge in sale of canned beers in off-licenses, people started to use the pub less frequently, preferring to take some beer home and watch the telly in the comfort of their own home.

The end of brewing in Grimsby (1968)

The decline of the fishing industry had begun, in Grimsby, the world's largest fishing port, people felt the pinch more than most. Public houses in the area of the town's fish docks were closing at an alarming pace. More were to follow when, in order to build the Cleethorpe Road flyover, demolition was necessary to clear the area where it was to be erected. In November 1967, it was announced that Hewitt's bottling plant would close on 8 December, with twenty workers being made redundant. There was no comment from the company; however, the fans were now driving the fire and complete closure was imminent.

"Hewitt's Brewery Closes Next Month – Official". So read the earth-shattering headlines of the Grimsby Telegraph of 14th March, 1968. Although the news was not totally unexpected, it still came as a shock to brewery workers and townsfolk alike. Mr TB Bourdillon, then Hewitt's MD, announced that brewing would cease on 19th April 1968. The ales would be recreated at Tadcaster in Yorkshire, with Hewitt's head brewer, Barry Peacock, overseeing the first run-through of beers in full scale production. Mr Bourdillon continued "Because of increasing costs and ageing plant, it would be uneconomical to refurbish the Tower Brewery". He stressed that the decision had nothing to do with the devaluation of the pound or the introduction of the breathalyser test on motorists. The bit of good news however, was that only around 20 staff would be made redundant and that the Pasture Street site would continue to be the company's headquarters; still trading as Hewitt Bros. Ltd.

Grimsby Evening Telegraph of 14 March 1968

Beer production in Grimsby in 1967/68 was around 100,000 barrels (1 barrel = 36 gallons) for a twelve month period. In early April 1968, the aforementioned Barry Peacock made the journey to Tadcaster, arriving at the Bass-Charrington brewhouse to be greeted by a "space-age" console of dials, gauges and buttons. The fully automated brewing process could be operated by one person within the glass sided, stainless steel unit.

Mr Peacock was a highly respected master brewer and well known within the industry. He inspected the materials for the brew and checked the stages of progress in order to ensure that standards be maintained. He was said to have been most impressed. Barry pressed a button and the first of the Yorkshire brewed, Grimsby-Lincolnshire beer was on its way. Mr Bourdillon claimed that Bass-Charrington produced a wide variety of beers to cater for local tastes and that, if anything, the Tadcaster brew would be even better than that which it had replaced.

Unfortunately, Barry Peacock's great effort was destined to be short-lived. Commonly, a large brewery that has taken over a smaller rival will reduce or delete the other brewery's beer range in favour of its own brews. While this is for no other than financial reasons the brewery will generally justify this by stating that the demand for the original beers has gone down (often because the beers are not on offer in the first instance).

Hewitt's beers – sorry, not available any more

Within a couple of years, Hewitt's ales had been replaced by the ubiquitous Brew X (Ten) and XXX Mild from Tadcaster. During this period, the high tower and brewing hall in Grimsby had been demolished, with some equipment being salvaged and reinstalled in the Bass-owned Stones's brewery in Sheffield. Hewitt's name had also been removed from all their former public houses as Bass, in their wisdom, took the opinion that the pub estate's name should be based on a brewery company which was in production. As Hewitt's no longer brewed, then the pubs should be badged under the title "Bass-Charrington". This was completed by around 1970.

Kegbuster - courtesy Bill Tidy, 2008

Page sponsored by Parkinson Arms, Mary Street, Scunthorpe

It's July 1970 and Britain has a new Conservative government, with Edward Heath in the Prime Minister's chair. It was not long before the country was plunged into chaos, with major strikes occurring throughout Heath's four years in office; the miners' and dockers' stoppages being particularly memorable when the UK was submerged into darkness. Electricity supplies to homes and workplaces were cut on a rotation basis. The streets were unlit (thank goodness it was the 1970's) and pubs that didn't serve beer through handpumps couldn't open, as a power supply was needed to operate the keg and lager dispensers. Oh, and wax candles were changing hands on a sort of black market basis!

November 1973 and it was Hewitt's driver and warehouse staff who had joined the millions of employees downing tools in a dispute over pay and conditions. Thomas Hewitt had, in the General Strike of 1926, avoided his business being affected by the withdrawal of labour with a few stern words to his staff. Not so this time. A series of one-day strikes over the run-up to Christmas made a serious dent in the pub trade as supplies of beer and lager dried up as the strike took hold. I recall going into the Freeman's Arms during this time and was delighted to see Bateman's ales on the bar. However, I wasn't so joyful when I couldn't get into my local pub, the New Empire which had to close because no supplies had been delivered. The dispute was resolved at the end of December 1973, with things returning to normal in January.

The Hewitt's maltings in Grimsby's Victoria Street had been out of use since 1968, when brewing ceased in Pasture Street. During its period of closure, the Victorian building had been put up for sale by the brewers at a price of around £27,000 - a snip compared to today's house prices. The maltings had been thought ripe for conversion to shops, offices and an auditorium. Even veteran actor Sir Bernard Miles (he of the "Looks good, tastes good and by golly it does you good!" Mackeson Stout TV advert) got in on the act, to raise a campaign in order to save what, in my opinion, was one of the finest of the industrial buildings that the town ever had.

Early 1970's view of Hewitt's maltings from Northwest, part of Sanders' maltings on left (courtesy NELC library)

Sadly, over the years, lead had been stripped from the roof, water had seeped through and the outer walls had started to bow. In January 1975, a couple of weeks after the maltings had been awarded "listed" status, a drunken youth had gained entry via an unsecured window and was thought to have lit a fire to keep himself warm. Unfortunately, the fire had got beyond his control and a huge blaze ensued, engulfing the building, with flames reaching a height of 100 feet. The maltings were gutted and the cost of restoration was said to be astronomical. As usual the answer was demolition and Grimsby lost yet another attractive historical building. The case against the youth was not proven.

Fire in the maltings, January 1975 (courtesy Grimsby Telegraph)

The 1970's misery continued. Labour Prime Minister Harold Wilson and his successor, James Callaghan had brought the country to its knees by 1978 – the "winter of discontent" and just to put the political balance right, the Liberal Party also had problems, with its leader, Jeremy Thorpe being accused of conspiring to murder his lover,

Page sponsored by Beeches Hotel, Grimsby, Tel: 01472 278830

Norman Scott. Mr Thorpe was later cleared of the charges.

Elsewhere, in another industry the great pub swap was taking place with Bass, John Smith and Tetley breweries exchanging pubs, where a near monopoly had occurred in some towns and cities. Hewitt's, now of course a part of Bass was involved in the Grimsby area, with some popular locals changing owners. The New Empire, Hope & Anchor, Cricketers and White Knight transferred to Tetley, whilst the Albion, Oak Tree and Yarborough Vaults were taken by John Smith's. There was a mixed reaction to the swaps. Some drinkers were pleased to get Tetley's real ale, whilst others were less than joyous to receive keg John Smith's in place of keg Brew Ten. The last pub swap had occurred about 35 years earlier during World War II, when restrictions were placed on beer being delivered outside a local area, due to fuel rationing etc.

This is where Hewitt's used to be ...

The end of the 70's saw a new government and a woman in charge of the UK. The good ship Hewitt's was sailing on its final voyage. The Pasture Street premises had been reduced to a distribution centre for Bass. Plans were in place to move from the Tower Brewery in Grimsby town centre to the outside of town in a former toilet roll factory on the Pyewipe industrial estate. The Pasture Street site was becoming very cramped and the introduction of huge articulated road trucks, delivering to the premises were causing problems – blocking roads and creating traffic jams in the vicinity.

By 1980 the move was complete and Hewitt's was no more. The unthinkable had happened and the brewery, cooperage and bottling store now stood empty, with the "For sale" signs attached to the brickwork. The Hewitt's trading area was now split, with the area to the north of the River Humber coming under Bass Yorkshire, administered from York, whilst the south was run from Sheffield under the William Stones banner. Stones Best Bitter was now on sale in the former Hewitt's pubs, with the pubs badged accordingly.

Hewitt's was gone but certainly not forgotten. In 1984, Stones Brewery decided to refurbish what was once the Hewitt's Brewery Tap, the Duke of Wellington in Pasture Street and transformed it into Hewitt's Tavern. It was totally gutted and reopened after a six week closure. Real ale had returned and so had popular licensees, husband and wife team, Geoff and Sylvia Milthorpe. Former MD, Peter Hewitt performed the unveiling of the signboard at the official opening and co-director, Arthur Matson pulled the first pint. The premises were literally stuffed inside and out with historic items, photographs and old adverts from Hewitt's. So impressed were the town's drinkers, that in 1985, the local branch of Campaign for Real Ale (CAMRA) bestowed upon it the prestigious "Pub of the Year" award. Lunches were available for between 60p and £1.60; Tavern Grills for £1.50 and even a Hewitt Burger for 60p. A pint of Stones' Best Bitter would cost you 74p and Best Mild 72p. The Tavern reverted to the Duke of Wellington in 1991, due to public demand (really?).

The Tower Brewery was demolished in 1985. The Crown Prosecution Service had purchased the land and new Crown Court rooms were built, whilst the huge bottling plant was knocked down around 2000 to make way for a road underpass. The cooperage however is still standing in 2008, awaiting long overdue restoration.

The derelict cooperage on Victoria Street in 2008 (photo by the author)

Page sponsored by Traditional Cobbler's Shop, Brereton Avenue, Grimsby

Part 2 – Hewitt's remembered

People, places, facts, anecdotes, myths and .... legends

The story, so far has been one of people doing business, making the headlines or both. What follows is a collection of more things Hewitt's – educating and entertaining ....

Rejuvenator

German-born Otto Overbeck was at one time head chemist at the brewery. He owned a house in the centre of Grimsby, close to the Bull Ring area and was the inventor of the "Overbeck Rejuvenator". He left the town to reside in Salcombe, Devon, where he established the Overbeck Museum and Gardens in an Edwardian mansion, set in six acres, containing landscaped shrubs, rare trees and dwarf plants, complemented by coloured stones and gravel. He died in 1938, aged 78 and in his will he had left his amazing home to the National Trust on condition that it remained in his name forever. In 1981, the Trust renamed it "Sharpitor" but quickly reverted to the original name. Why?

Because a clause in the will stipulated that should the name be changed then the property had to be sold, with the proceeds going to Grimsby Council to build a new swimming pool. It wasn't sold and is still there today. Oh, and of course Grimsby got no cash.

Otto Overbeck in mid-1930's ad for the Rejuvenator

"Just what is the Overbeck Rejuvenator?" I hear you asking. This was a device dispensing electric shocks – it was claimed that these would make its user feel fresh and invigorated. Today's TENS machines (transcutaneous electric nerve stimulator) appear to operate on a similar principle. The original apparatus is apparently on display in the Overbeck Museum. Like Vivian Hewitt, Otto became more famous (and wealthier) when disengaged from the brewing industry.

Long hours and hard times

Fred Walker of Grimsby reminisces about his years spent at Grimsby's best-known brewery and the hazards of the job. Here Mr Walker tells us of his experiences of working at Hewitt Brothers.

When I started work at the bottling stores in Queen Street in 1941, I was 16 years of age and I didn't think much to the job. I even told my mother on the first day that I wasn't going back. I not only returned but stayed for 45 years, including Army service during the Second World War.

"In those early days some horse-drawn transport was used for making local deliveries. This was because of fuel rationing and whilst the work was laborious for the draymen, it was no less tiring for the bottling store staff. Health and safety measures were not paramount and it was difficult for young people to lift some of the containers. The draymen developed definite skills when handling the larger barrels but for beginners the prospect was daunting.

A gallon of beer weighs 10 pounds and the largest wooden barrel contained 36 gallons. Other containers held eighteen gallons and eleven gallons. Wooden cases which we handled in the store, housed two dozen pints of beer (later reduced to one dozen – the author) and there were also smaller cases that contained 24 half-pint bottles.

Page sponsored by Sandra & Steve Tucker

52

Gloves and safety footwear were non-existent in the early years and accidents frequently happened. Cuts to fingers caused by broken bottles were a common hazard and wooden splinters easily pierced vulnerable flesh. The cases had a wire binding which was pinned to the wood and sometimes, when a case became worn, a metal staple would rip into an exposed finger.

L. to r.: Stephen Burt (manager drinks & tobacco retail), unknown, E. Shepherd (bottling dept manager), blind man: Larry Ward (crates repairman). Donald Burt, MD (father of Stephen) circa 1955 (courtesy Grimsby Telegraph)

The girls in the store, who worked on the filling machines, had to be wary of exploding bottles. The job was tedious and the hours long but the girls always seemed to be cheerful. Perhaps it's strange to relate that despite the low wages and wearisome routine, people stayed there for many years. Numerous lasting friendships were formed among the workforce and several romances blossomed. The girl who was to become my wife came to work at Hewitt's and I often wonder what would have happened if I hadn't gone back on that first day. Was it fate?

Staff party, early 1960's (photo from collection of Malcolm Beaumont)

Of course working conditions did improve with the advent of forklifts, the production of plastic cases and the introduction of metal kegs but that was many years later. Safety regulations were eventually imposed and they are now a requirement in the majority of industries.

Hewitt's Brewery no longer exists but memories still survive of hard times, of friendship and affection, of starting to work and doing 48 hours for 20 shillings (£1) a week. Things had to get better but glass bottles still shatter and a gallon of ale still weighs ten pounds!"

Page sponsored by Fairway Newsagent, The Fairway, Waltham, Grimsby

Beer boat

A little known story was told to us by Mrs Helen Davidson of Cleethorpes. Helen's father, William Cowie, joined Hewitt's in 1934/35 but not as a brewery worker or publican. He was, in fact Chief Engineer of what was known as Hewitt's Beer Boat.

The Gambrinus was a steam-driven barge which was loaded with casks and bottles filled with beer from the Tower Brewery. It was berthed in the Riverhead at the rear of the Victoria street maltings, across the road from the Royal Oak public house, which was also owned by the brewers. The barge would sail twice a week, taking its cargo to Doncaster and Gainsborough. Helen did not know of the final destination but Hewitt's had depots in both towns and so it is a fair assumption that the beer was heading there.

No doubt the crew of four - skipper, mate, deckhand and engineer brought the empties back but I wonder if they managed to collect the penny deposit on all the returned bottles? Probably not! Helen would occasionally join the outward trip but as the barge had no guest accommodation, she had to return by train.

William was in the Royal Naval Reserves and at the outbreak of World War II he was "called up" to fight for

King and Country. Upon his return to "Civvy Street" after the cessation of hostilities in 1945, he learned to his horror that the barge runs had ceased and been replaced by motor lorries. He went on to be chief engineer on the "liverboat", which was a supply vessel servicing the Grimsby Docks. Sadly, he died in 1948 and unfortunately there seem to be no photographic record of the barge but what a fascinating story and thanks to Helen Davidson for telling it.

Smashing time - Shattering time

The peace of the hot summer of 1970 was shattered, when in June, a mysterious person nicknamed 'The Phantom' would, in the dead of night, mount his bicycle, arm himself with a quantity of old house bricks and proceed to attack pubs owned by Hewitt's; smashing as many windows as he could. He even went on to smash windows of the Tower Brewery. He was eventually apprehended. Many theories abound as to why he did it; the most popular was that as an ex-employee he had a grudge against the company or that he was enraged at the increased price of a pint of beer earlier that year. Nothing changes does it?

A spate of vandalism had been reported in the Scunthorpe area, with a breakage of several vehicle windscreens by unknown missiles, possibly rifle bullets but the assailants remained a mystery. However, another incident occurred in the Hull area, involving two Grimsby men returning home in a lorry from Hull. The occupants – Fred Read and Bill Tuplin were employed as draymen for Hewitt Bros. Ltd. Mr Read explained how he was driving a six-ton Hewitt's dray along Boothferry Road in Hull, "When I heard a slight thud and the windscreen suddenly shattered." "I think we were shot at, although nothing penetrated the glass", he added. Luckily both men were uninjured in the attack.

(from the Grimsby Evening Telegraph, 7th June 1952)

Draymen delivering barrels to the Humber Hotel, Grimsby in the 1950's
(courtesy Grimsby Telegraph)

Payday

In 1956, a drayman would earn around £6 for a 40 hour working week. A similar amount was earned by a 16 year old office junior in 1968, the year that brewing ceased at Hewitt's. Average earnings for the broad spectrum of Hewitt's employees were thought to be between £10 and £20 per week in the late 1960's.

Draymen at the Market Hotel, Grimsby, 1950's (courtesy Grimsby Telegraph)

Page sponsored by Peggy's Diner, Jackson Place, Humberston

Night out

Fancy a night out in a Hewitt's pub in 1955? Hewitt's Best Bitter: one shilling and two pence (6p today) per pint; Brown Ale: ninepence halfpenny (4p) per pint; half-pint bottle of Guinness: one shilling and four pence (7p); half-pint bottle of Tuborg lager: one shilling and seven pence (8p); HB Whiff's cigar: eight pence (3p); 20 Benson & Hedges Super Virginia cigarettes: four shillings and threepence (21p); 10 Woodbines or Park Drive cigarettes: one and fourpence-halfpenny (7p); Smith's crisps: threepence (1½p) per packet; roasted salted peanuts: sixpence (2½p) per large packet; twopence (1p) small.

This is what your average night out would cost in 1955 and now (2008):

	1955	2008
6 pints of bitter	36p	£15 (2.50 per pint average)
10 Park Drive Cigarettes	7p	£2.50
1 packet of crisps	1½p	50p
1 packet of nuts	1p	50p
total	45½p	£18.50

Good pint, bad pint!

George Muir (whose stepfather Norman was the boilerman at the brewery for a number of years) remembers when he was a youth in the 1950's and 60s, how he and his mates would go on a pub crawl, dressed in their sharp Italian suits, visiting as many a Hewitt's outlet. He recalls how the ale would vary from pub to pub. At one or two hostelries, a decent pint was guaranteed; however, in a fair number of others it was not. "When Hewitt's ale was good, it was very good but when it was bad, you knew about it and didn't touch it", George said. There was some rhyming slang about in those days. Think of being sick and match it with Hewitt's!

Advertisements from 1939 and 1940

That said, Hewitt's won many gold, silver and bronze medals over the years, for the quality of their beers. The accolades were awarded both in this country and internationally. A small selection of the "gongs" can, at the time of writing (2008) be viewed on display in the Duke of Wellington pub on Grimsby's Pasture Street.

Phil Ellis, owner of Fulstow Brewery, Louth revealed that it would have been down to the cellar housekeeping in those days, as there was no temperature control, beer pipes were made of silver and cleaning fluid was unheard of. Running cold water and washing soda through the pipes would have been normal practice.

"Beer is made the same way at all breweries", Phil said but it is what happens after it is put into barrels and sent to various pubs that things can go amiss. Beer lines are now made of nylon; easily cleaned and relatively cheap to replace. Cellars are usually chilled and a wide range of cleaning materials is readily available. Still, down to cellarmanship is the thought for the day though.

A tale of the unexpected - Hewitt's on television

Hart to Hart – a US-imported TV series starred Robert Wagner and Stephanie Powers as a millionaire businessman and his glamorous wife who, in their spare time were amateur sleuths. The series was a worldwide hit during the 1980's and the highlight of the 100 or so episodes was the appearance of a Hewitt's wall plaque, displaying the red circle and 'H' logo. In a key scene during one programme, the Hewitt's sign stole the show; outshining the supporting actors by miles!!

The action took place in an American lounge bar. Just what the episode was all about, I have no idea but the acting of Mr and Mrs Hart's dog "Freeway" was something else as he almost upstaged the sign by a long chalk.

The logo

Not everyone is aware but the Hewitt's most famous logo, the red circle (introduced in the mid 1950's), is in fact an upright barrel graphic with two squares cut out at the top and bottom, thus forming the letter 'H'. A simple but striking design, it is still effective in the 21st century- it was known in the trade as the 'Barrel H'.

A succession of Hewitt's logos – 'barrel' on right

Page sponsored by Thomas & Zoe Osborne and Ben Hough – the future of real ale!

Name that tune

Janet Muir recalls the time when she worked at the Hewitt's-owned and sadly long-demolished Ship Hotel, which stood in Flottergate, Grimsby (now covered by part of the Freshney Place shopping centre). Allegedly, during the 1960's, a couple of highly successful jazz bands stayed there whilst appearing at a local 'live' venue. They were at the height of their popularity; riding the waves of the then Hit Parade and guesting on such TV shows as 'Ready, Steady, Go' and 'Top of the Pops'. They had a reputation for being rather boisterous (as popular beat groups are) and on a particular occasion they became rather too raunchy, which landed them with a blanket ban from all Hewitt's establishments throughout the country. Janet cannot recall which famous band it was but you can form your own opinion as to which alleged entertainers caused the mayhem. You may find yourself '.. in Moscow', '.. on the shore', '.. a stranger at midnight' by doing so …

Place the face

Some well-known names and faces had a Hewitt's connection over the years. Dame Madge Kendal (née Margaret Shafto Robertson, 1848 – 1935), a celebrated Victorian and Edwardian actress was born in a coffee

Page sponsored by Wetherspoon's Yarborough Hotel, Grimsby Station Approach

house on Cleethorpe Road, Grimsby. Hewitt's bought the premises in 1887, promptly demolished and rebuilt it as the Railway Hotel. A "Blue Plaque" commemorating Dame Madge's birth was affixed to the wall in the 1940's and said to be the only Blue Plaque ever displayed in the town.

The Railway Hotel, Grimsby circa 1964 (courtesy Grimsby Telegraph)

The hotel was demolished in 1966/67 in order to make way for the flyover. The Royal Hotel across the road also suffered the same fate. The Royal was home to actress Patricia Hodge, star of Rumpole, Inspector Morse etc., whose parents ran the hotel for Hewitt Brothers.

In Freeman Street – an area famous for its pubs and shops – the Freemans Arms was, in 1953 to see its most famous landlord installed. Billy Cairns, a former Grimsby Town footballer took the reins and steered the pub for twenty-odd years. Billy's son Mike took over for a short period in the late 1970's, leaving to pursue a different career. The pub is still referred to as "Cairns's" and in the 1980's, the lounge area was renamed "Cairns's bar".

Anthony Crosland, MP for Grimsby 1959-1977 was Foreign Secretary during Harold Wilson and James Callaghan's reign as Labour Prime Minister. During a tour of Hewitt's brewery, he was alleged to have promised to do all that he could to keep Grimsby's biggest local employers in the town. He may well have done but we all know the eventual outcome. Enough said. He died in 1977.

The Royal Hotel, Grimsby, early 1960's (courtesy Grimsby Telegraph)

Freddie Frinton (1909-1968), whose real name was Freddie Coo (some older sources quote Bittener or Hargate), was born in Grimsby. His father was a

Page sponsored by Monarco Restaurant & Chippy (est. 1948), Alexandra Rd, Cleethorpes fisherman and Freddie worked briefly on the fish dock before embarking on a comedy variety career. He had his own TV sitcom "Meet the Wife", in which he co-starred with Thora Hird in the 1960's, playing the role of a layabout plumber Fred Blacklock. Freddie's most famous role was playing a drunk in the theatre and on TV variety shows, which he did for 30 years. Ironically, Freddie hardly touched a drop of alcohol but was often seen in the Grimsby Hewitt's pubs during his many visits during his "resting" periods. Only known to an older generation in the UK he is a cult performer on German and Scandinavian TV every New Year's Eve with his hilarious performance of drunken butler James in the "Dinner for One" sketch. This may be viewed online via YouTube (2 versions available). Give it a look.

Grimbarian Freddie Frinton in 1963 German TV production
of Dinner for One' (photo: Norddeutscher Rundfunk)

Lincoln Arms, Grimsby early 1960's (courtesy Grimsby Telegraph)

Sir Richard Attenborough, the world famous actor and film director made a couple of visits to the Hewitt's hostelry, the Clee Park Hotel during the mid 1970's. He collected cheques on behalf of the Muscular Dystrophy group of Great Britain. Landlords Telfer (better known as Jock) and Mary McRobert were well known on the local pub scene, having run several Hewitt's pubs prior to the Clee Park. They were also great charity fundraisers and Sir Richard collected £14,000 raised by the couple, their staff and customers. Big Jock was often seen walking his dog in the morning by standing in the side doorway of the Clee Park, his dog on a long lead walking to and fro on the pavement taking his constitution. But fear not, for Jock also exercised the dog later in the day with a good, brisk walk. Jock died in the early 1990's.

Page sponsored by Tetney Road Service Station, Humberston. Tel. 01472 813330

Charles Ekberg, a well known local journalist, broadcaster and keen Grimsby Town FC fan was also a big champion of Hewitt's. He would often be seen in the Pestle & Mortar or the Wheatsheaf Hotel, quaffing the best of Grimsby's ale. Such a devotee was he that at one time he was Publicity Officer for the brewers and to his credit tried in vain to persuade the new parent company, Bass to retain the Hewitt's identity and trading area. Sadly, in the early 1980's his battle was lost and the pubs, drays and brewery were badged under the "William Stones" legend. Stones, based in Sheffield had also become part of the Bass Empire and their trading area was extended into the former Hewitt's region, resulting in the complete loss of the Hewitt's local name and historical status.

Awayday

Going on holiday or having a day trip? Then you might wish to visit one or more of former Hewitt's pubs which were spread around the region. Some were brought under their ownership as a result of takeovers and mergers. Hewitt's eventually owned pubs stretching from North and South Yorkshire through North Nottinghamshire, North Derbyshire and throughout Lincolnshire. They include: The Buck Inn, Hunmanby, near Whitby; The Cross Keys, Goodramgate and The Bay

Horse, Gillygate, both in York; The Greyhorse Inn, Barnsley; The Fox Inn, Stainforth; The Strugglers Inn and City Hotel, Lincoln; The Royal Crescent, Filey; The Market Tavern and Rose Hotel, Hull; Hanover House, Sheffield; The Bay Horse, Arnold, Nottingham; The Newmarket, Louth; The Black Bull and Horse & Groom, both Doncaster; Station Hotel, Scunthorpe; Flixborough Inn, Flixborough; The Drovers' Call, Gainsborough and The Great Northern, Boston.

Probably the best known of their pubs is the former Anchor Inn at Brandy Wharf, Waddingham, Lincolnshire. Located between Grimsby and Gainsborough on the B1205, it is on a bank of the River Ancholme and is something of a unique pub, for it no longer sells draught beer but specialises in cider. The Brandy Wharf Cider Centre as it is now called offers a range of ciders from far and wide, including its own products made with fruit grown from its own orchard. In an idyllic setting, with camping facilities available, try it sometime but please don't drink and drive. If you would like to get the feel of a Hewitt's pub in the 1950/60's, then why not visit the National Fishing Heritage Centre, close to the shopping area in the heart of Grimsby, where a mock-up of a popular town pub has been created.

Hewitt's scholarly facts

Malcolm Beaumont was a student brewer at Hewitt's during the mid-1950's. He has provided us with some rather more studious facts for the "serious" reader about the brewery.

There were 15 storage tanks and 16 coldwater tanks in the bottling store, all of stainless steel and alloy. The 29 fermenting vessels in the brewery were of various sizes constructed using Yorkshire slate, stainless steel and alloy. It had its own well and water was extracted for brewing from beneath the Pasture Street premises. Malcolm said that, at times the brewing staff feared that the fresh water well could become contaminated by seawater filtering through at exceptionally high tides from the nearby River Humber. However, hard work and determination by the workers prevented this from happening.

Mr Beaumont also provided some more facts. The main beers produced were as follows:

XXXX Dark Mild	ABV 3.2%
BB	ABV 3.5%
HB	ABV 3.9%
Oatmeal Stout	ABV 3.9%
Export	ABV 5.2%
Strong Ale	ABV 7.3%

Like to know how the wood was curved to make the barrels? Well, simply put, the lengths of wood were erected around the barrel base and steel hoops placed around to hold them together. Wood chippings and sawdust were put inside which were then set alight. The resultant heat caused the wood to warp and was pushed into shape by the barrel makers known as coopers. The top was then fitted and sealed and there you have your beer barrel or cask. A very skilled occupation with years of experience was required to achieve the end product.

Meeting at Guinness School of Brewing, Dublin 1956. Back row: Hewitt's student brewer Malcolm (Beaumont) in the middle

Hewitt's trading area covered over 5000 square miles and the brewing process was in operation virtually seven days a week, with their fleet of 39 delivery drays constantly on the road supplying the 400-plus pubs and many off-licenses with their wares.

Malcolm later moved to London to work at the Wenlock Brewery Co. (then Bass-owned) in Shoreditch. Sadly, that has since closed and (again) the buildings have been demolished. Malcolm now lives in retirement in Lincolnshire.

Work in the cooperage

Hewitt's Ale – set in music

(Tune – "Villikins and his Dinah")
Alf Ludlam of Grimsby sent us this song. Written by Bill
Meek and John Conolly and first performed in the Duke
of Wellington around 1962, it is reproduced with their
kind permission.
NB: if you don't know the tune, read it as a poem.

I once knew a weakling of seven stone ten,
Who daren't take his shirt off beside other men
He wrote to Charles Atlas and told him his sad tale
Who sent him a crateful of Hewitt's best ale

CHORUS: It won't fail, it can't fail,
That ubiquitous liquid they call Hewitt's ale.

If you've got no family and your wife wants six,
There's a sure way out of this terrible fix.
Go down to the local, take with you a pail,
And sup down four gallons of Hewitt's best ale.

Repeat chorus

If your drains are clogged up and won't run any more,
And the water is creeping all over the floor.
Should the usual methods prove of no avail,
Pour down a bottle of Hewitt's best ale.

Repeat chorus

My sister's fiancé said "Dear it's no go,
Your best friends will tell you that you've got B.O."
But now she feels fresh where before she felt stale,
She fills up her bathtub with Hewitt's best ale.

Repeat chorus

A lady went out for a ride in her car.
She ran out of petrol, the garage was far.
A Grimbarian passing said "Don't look so pale!
It'll run off a bottle of Hewitt's best ale."

Repeat chorus

If your natural functions are proving a strain,
And you've been to the doc's again and again.
If the syrup of figs and the senna pods fail,
Try half-a-teaspoon of Hewitt's best ale.

Repeat chorus

Page sponsored by

GRIMSBY CLEETHORPES LIONS CLUB
Lion Alan King – Treasurer
28 Mill Road, Cleethorpes, N. E. Lincs, DN35 8JA

Lament

A poem by Anne E Watson first published in the Grimsby Telegraph in April 1985.

Brick by brick I saw today

Our wonderful heritage thrown away

How could they think of pulling it down?

When for two hundred years it's graced our town

Hewitt's the brewery should never have gone

That well known façade deserved to live on

And with Pasture Street's loss to me it's plain

My Grimsby will never be quite the same.

Class B1 4-6-0 No 61166 hauling a Daybrook-Cleethorpes excursion near West Victoria Street / Pasture Street, May 1961 brewery in the background (photo: John Willerton)

Two beer recipes to try

Former Grimsby residents, David & Karen Edwards have provided a couple of beer recipes for your pleasure. If you can't find any Hewitt's ale (if you can then let me know!), you can replace it with one of your favourites. Try them out and I'm sure that you'll enjoy them.

Hewitt's Ale & Cheese Soup

Ingredients:

1 tbsp	olive oil
2	large onions
½ tsp	brown sugar
1 pint	beer, light in colour
1 pint	chicken stock
	salt, pepper
	a handful of breadcrumbs
	knob of butter
	handful of grated Gruyère or Parmesan cheese

Heat the oil and butter together in a large saucepan. Finely slice the onions and place in the pan on a high heat, making sure that the onions are well coated with the oil and butter but don't overbrown. Put the lid on the pan and simmer but keep stirring for a few minutes. Add the sugar, beer and stock. Add a pinch of salt and pepper, stir well and bring to the boil. Add breadcrumbs, simmer for 20 minutes. The ingredients can then be pureed before being returned to the pan to ensure consistency. It's now ready for pouring into bowls. Sprinkle with cheese and serve with wholemeal bread or French breadstick.

Hewitt's Ale & Beef Loaf

Ingredients:

1	French loaf or small bloomer (circa 450g / 1 lb.)
tbsp	tomato puree
2 or 3	tomatoes (fresh or tinned)
1 oz.	chopped streaky bacon (cooked)
8 oz.	minced beef (250g)
2 tspn	mixed herbs or oregano
1/2 pint	beer

Cut the loaf in half lengthways. Scoop out the breadcrumbs from the middle, leaving two bread shells. Mix the breadcrumbs and remaining ingredients together in a saucepan with the beer and cook until a pate-like savoury mixture is formed. Pack the mixture into the breadshells and place into the lower part of the oven at gas mark 5 (190 to 200 degrees centigrade) for about 20 minutes (check loaf with skewer). You can either serve in two halves or put the loaf back together and cut into slices or chunks. Minced lamb or turkey may be used instead of beef.

The pub gaffers

There have been scores of pub landlords who have worked for Hewitt's over the decades. Here are just a few of the well-known "gaffers" who have kept the beer flowing. Apologies to those who haven't been mentioned.

Ray & Annie Barker

Sid & Mabel Bascomb

Clarrie Bateman

Les Bell

Fred Bishop

Jack Busby (reputed to be Hewitt's longest serving gaffer)

Billy Cairns

Ernie Ferrier

Sam Flatman

Stan George

Roly Godfrey

Mick Godfrey

George Gorringe

Bill Hallam

Jim Hutson

Les Jepson

George (Ginger) Lane

Jock McRobert

Geoff Milthorpe

George & Violet Mogg

Joe Moran

Tom Parkinson

Eric & Joy Reynolds

Tom & Nellie Taylor

Sonny & Connie Turner

Jack & Alma Wigglesworth

and last but not least a gentleman with the splendid name of

Fred Woodbine!

Fancy a takeaway?

Like for most brewers, the off-license was an integral part of the business and more often than not was attached to a particular pub. However, the stand-alone shops selling wines, spirits, bottled and draught beers, crisps, nuts and sweets were often run by independent shop owners, as they still are today. Some, of course were acquired by brewery companies. Hewitt's owned a fair few, either outright or as landowners; charging rent to the tenant. Here are a few that some may recall:

Grimsby: Chapman Street; Garden Street; Flottergate; Rutland Street; Newmarket Street; Victor Street

Skegness: High Street; Church Road; Roman Bank

Scunthorpe: Cottage Beck Road; Crosby Road; Ashby High Street; Old Brumby Street

Lincoln: Shakespeare Street; St. Andrew Street; Little Bargate Street; Oakfield Street

Gainsborough: Spital Terrace; Asquith Street

Hull: Constable Street; West Dock Avenue.

Others were located in New Waltham, South Killingholme, Barton upon Humber, Alford, Tuxford (Nottinghamshire) and Clowne (North Derbyshire).

Hush! Hush!

An intriguing story was told to us by Cleethorpes resident Miriam Wickes. Mrs Wickes' late first husband, George Victor Waller (known as Vic, see appendix for photo), was a painter and decorator for Hewitt's. During a major refit of the County Hotel, Immingham in 1946, Vic discovered under some linoleum (floor covering) in one of the rooms, a number of letters addressed to Earl Louis Mountbatten (1900-1979). The hotel was commandeered by the Forces during World War II and used as naval offices and accommodation during the hostilities. Lord Mountbatten visited the hotel on many occasions in his role of Admiral of the Fleet. Apparently, the letters were never opened and were returned to the War Office, "contents unknown"

Lord Mountbatten was killed in 1979, aged 78, by an IRA bomb on his yacht in County Sligo, Ireland. A bistro bar is dedicated to the "Last Viceroy of India" at the County Hotel and named "The Mountbatten Bar". Vic Waller later worked in Hewitt's warehouse and sadly died in 1984 at the age of 66.

Horse and beer!

The Lord Raglan pub was situated on the corner of Orwell Street and Riby Square, Grimsby, just opposite the entrance to the famous fish docks. The premises did not have a wines & spirits licence for most of its existence. Demolished circa 1964, the pub only ever sold beer. One of its most famous customers was a white horse called Ned. A local fish carter named Tom would steer his cart - pulled by Ned - to the Raglan. Tom would then open the pub doors so that Ned could get his daily pint of Hewitt's ale, served in a special oversized beer mug. Ned wouldn't move until he had finished his pint! It was Tom's turn for a pint or three after Ned had finished

The Lord Raglan in the 1940's, landlady Violet Mogg (centre), courtesy Grimsby
Telegraph; inset: exterior of the pub

and meanwhile his horse waited patiently outside for his owner to stagger back to the cart. Tom wasn't worried about driving back as the horse knew the routine well enough. This scenario happened six days a week, Monday till Saturday for quite a long period. Just what they both did on a Sunday without their daily fix of Hewitt's Best Bitter is anyone's guess.

Impression of a horse dray by Abigail Zambon

Myths and legends

Breweries and public houses have a certain romance about them don't they? None more so than when visiting old pubs throughout the country and hearing the ghost stories. Hewitt's establishments were no exception to these.

The Tower Brewery was said to be haunted by an ex-worker who died in an accident on site and pubs formerly owned by Hewitt's which allegedly had eerie happenings included the White Hart in Grimsby's Old Market Place (the oldest pub in town), where apparitions were seen floating from bar to bar. The New Empire in Grimsby's Runswick Road, where a young girl dressed in Victorian clothing was seen regularly on a Sunday morning. Probably the most famous haunting still occurs at the Corporation Arms on Freeman Street, Grimsby. It is believed to be the ghost of Mrs Maria Drayton, a former landlady who perished in 1926 after jumping from an upper floor in order to escape a serious fire which had begun at the foot of the stairs. There were regular attempts at flooding the cellar by turning on the cold water taps. Lager and "keg" beer pumps cease to function. However, she leaves untouched the handpumps which serve real ale (what a wise ghost!).

I conclude the ghost thingy with a tale of my own. Whilst visiting the ex-Hewitt's inn, the Wheatsheaf in Louth, Lincs. On 19th January 2008 I was standing in the bar speaking to some friends, when I felt someone brush past behind me. I turned to see who it was but saw only the fireplace, with no room for a person to pass by. I asked people sitting close to the area if they had seen anyone and "no" was the reply. I was informed by a regular that the pub is reputed to be haunted.

Did these things really occur? Are you a believer? The truth is out there!!

The conveyor connecting brewery and bottling plant, Pasture Street
(computer adaptation by Rafael Marsh, courtesy Brian Clark)

Finally, legend has it that a pipe used to connect the brewery to the tap house across the road, namely the Duke of Wellington pub and that this so-called pipe was connected to the handpump on the bar top. Now, I don't believe this for one moment; however, a roller type conveyor belt did exist, crossing Pasture Street at a height of about 30 feet, it connected the brewery with the bottling plant. It conveyed crates of bottles to and fro for cleaning, filling and storing ready for delivery.

And finally ....!

A man walks into a Hewitt's pub with a pig under his arm. The barman says "Where did you get that thing from?"

"I won it in a raffle" replied the pig.

(Kay Clifford)

Epilogue

In the first part of this book you could read how Hewitt's of Grimsby became history in a matter of years after a large company had acquired and closed the brewery - for the sake of having pubs to sell its own beers in. It would be unfair to finish without a few small but important remarks ....

As far as the giants and predators are concerned: in a case of history repeating Belgian beer giant Interbrew bought the brewing sides of Whitbread and also Bass (plc), the latter for a mere £2.3 billion in 2000. As a company operating at this level Interbrew were no strangers to the 'murder and acquisition' business with a track record of buying and closing down reputable breweries in Belgium.

This deal would have left two thirds of brewing in Great Britain in the hands of Interbrew and Scottish & Newcastle Breweries. The Office of Fair Trade instructed Interbrew to sell Bass. In 2002 a large US brewer (whose name we do not wish to mention) bought the Bass brewing interests from Interbrew who made a substantial loss in the process. As a matter of irony the brewing of Draught Bass moved within Burton-upon-Trent to archrival Marston's in 2005. Production of cask ale at the old Bass brewery itself has ceased.

In spring 2000 the North East Lincolnshire branch of CAMRA (Campaign for Real Ale) had arranged for a Hewitt's beer to be recreated from an original recipe, courtesy of Steve Wellington, now Head Brewer at the White Shield Brewery in Burton-upon-Trent.

The Hewitt's Ale went down a storm at the CAMRA Cleethorpes Beer Festival that year, with three barrels being consumed by festival drinkers, easily outselling other beers on sale.

September 2006 saw the bicentenary of the opening of the original Hewitt's brewhouse in 1806. Again, a Hewitt's beer, brewed to an original recipe was produced, this time more locally by Phil Ellis at the Fulstow Brewery, Louth in order to celebrate the occasion. I personally had commissioned a small number of die-cast, Hewitt's liveried model drays, to add to the anniversary.

It is now 2008 and 40 years since the Hewitt's Tower Brewery ceased production in April 1968. In order to mourn its passing and in the true spirit of the Hewitt family, we have decided to produce this book as something of a souvenir to the former Grimsby brewers, with ALL profits going to St. Andrew's Hospice Appeal, in order to assist in the wonderful work that the Grimsby Hospice does for people from all around the former Hewitt trading area. We hope that you have enjoyed reading the book and that you learned things (as I certainly did whilst researching) that you never knew about Grimsby's famous brewing dynasty. All that we need now is another Grimsby brewery to take its place. So "Cheers!" and please drink sensibly. Oh, and finally, thanks for buying the book.

Grimsby branch of Campaign for Real Ale (CAMRA) presenting Pub of the Year 1984/85 award to Geoff Millthorpe, Hewitt's Tavern (now Duke of Wellington), courtesy Grimsby Telegraph

Appendix

This section contains some pictures of interest (mainly places and people) that could not be used in the earlier part of this book:

'Vic' Waller, Hewitt's painter (right, see p. 79), colleague on L unknown

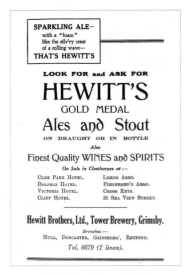

Hewitt's ad circa 1930's

Hewitt's workers' football team 1940's. Back L to r: Brian Rogerson, Arthur Furneaux, Ted Howlett, Tom Hand, Albert Maddems, Gerry Pearson. Front L to r: Doug Abernethie, Les Cook, George Rising, Bob Leggot, Harry Holliday. Photo courtesy George Rising

Demolished Hewitt's pubs and Overbeck House

Clockwise from bottom left: Otto Overbeck's house, Flottergate; Oil Miller's Arms, East Marsh Street; Black Swan, Victoria Street; Robin Hood, Albion Street; Honest Lawyer, Kent Street; Bricklayer's Arms, Nelson Street; Old King's Head, Victoria Street (all buildings in Grimsby)

Hewitt's pubs, early 20th century

Top: Brewery Inn, Retford, bottom: Carpenter's Arms, Fiskerton nr Lincoln
(scanned film plates, courtesy Miriam Wickes)

Acknowledgments

The author wishes to thank the following people and institutions for their help and contributions:

Bill Tidy
Abigail Zambon
Brian Ashwell
Peter Chapman (special thanks)
Dennis Lister
Martin Clausen
Linda Roberts
Staff of Grimsby Public Library
Grimsby Telegraph Archive

Michelle Lalor, Editor, Grimsby Telegraph
Geoff Millthorpe
Malcolm Beaumont
Jenny Bowden
Tony Kyle
Miriam Wickes
Claire Brown
Alan Walker
Phil Ellis
Brewery History Society

... the sponsors for their generosity

Sources of information

Modest Millionaire by William Hywell
A Century of British Brewers (Norman Barber, Brewery History Society)
Beer – The story of the pint (Martin Cornell)
NELC Grimsby Public Library Archive
Donny Drinker, newsletter of Doncaster branch Campaign for Real Ale (CAMRA)

Index of people and institutions

All profits from the sale of this book are donated to St Andrews Hospice, Grimsby

The hospice cares for adults and children from North East Lincolnshire (and beyond), who suffer from progressive life-limiting illnesses (e.g. cancer, advanced emphysema, some neurological conditions, lymphoedema) and require palliative treatment. The aim is improve the patient's quality of life by providing specialist medical and nursing care in a safe, welcoming environment for in- and outpatients. Help and support are also available for patients' families and carers. The services are free of charge to patients, St Andrews relies mainly on donations.

http://www.standrewshospice.com/

St Andrews Hospice
Peaks Lane
Grimsby
DN32 9RP

Disclaimer

The author has taken every effort to identify the original sources of text and images reproduced in this book and credit these. The author does not accept responsibility for errors or inaccuracies. In the unlikely case that content from an uncredited third party appears to be included this does not imply that the author claims intellectual ownership. An updated list of corrections and clarifications can be accessed at http://www.hewittsbook.co.uk.

Printed by Spectrum Print, Cleethorpes